RECOVERED

by the grace of GOD

DONALD MILBOCKER

RECOVERED BY THE GRACE OF GOD

iUniverse books may be ordered through booksellers or by contacting:

iUniverse
1663 Liberty Drive
Bloomington, IN 47403
www.iuniverse.com
1-800-Authors (1-800-288-4677)

Because of the dynamic nature of the Internet, any web addresses or links contained in this book may have changed since publication and may no longer be valid. The views expressed in this work are solely those of the author and do not necessarily reflect the views of the publisher, and the publisher hereby disclaims any responsibility for them.

Any people depicted in stock imagery provided by Getty Images are models, and such images are being used for illustrative purposes only. Certain stock imagery © Getty Images.

ISBN: 978-1-5320-7650-3 (sc)
ISBN: 978-1-5320-7651-0 (e)

Print information available on the last page.

iUniverse rev. date: 06/06/2019

The whole purpose of writing this book is to be helpful to the reader who may have a problem with alcohol or someone who thinks they may have a problem with alcohol or other substance. Or may have something else blocking them from the sun light of the Spirit or even if they want to improve their relationship with our Creator.

I pray that the reader finds comfort in these words and that God's grace Comes over them and helps them to better understand his will for them.

Amen

Medical definition of alcoholism

The alcoholic cannot control the consumption of alcohol. When an alcoholic drinks alcohol an overwhelming desire or craving to want more occurs, that they cannot control. They want it all the time, they think about it all the time, no matter what harm it may bring to them, to their personal life, their family life, their work. Left untreated they become dependent on it. The only Solution for them is complete abstinence.

CHAPTER ONE
Alcohol Insanity

I was born on a small farm in Michigan in 1960, I was number six, out of seven children. My Father was a hardworking man, who loved his home-made beer and whiskey. Drinking was a big social event, everybody had alcohol, and everybody was drinking alcohol. I started drinking with sips of my Dad's beer at an early age, everyone thought it was cute that I would take a few sips of my dad's beer and stumble around and fall down. I have to say it felt pretty good to me at the time, it was something I never experienced before.

That behavior went on all the way up to when I became a teenager, at thirteen, fourteen, and fifteen, I started to steal my dad's homemade beer, and sometimes his whiskey, and I would take it and hide it, so I could drink it when no one would know. He always had a lot of it, so he never missed it. During the summer months after we got all our crops picked and put away in the barn and bins, I would go help the neighbor's pick their crops and get them put away. They would pay me a few dollars for helping them, but almost always they would give me a bottle of their homemade beer or whiskey to give to my father. I loved that part of it, because that would give me another bottle I could stash somewhere. Living on a farm there is a lot of good hiding places to be found. Finally I turned sixteen, it was late November, and soon I would be able to get my driver's license.

1

That's ok I had a lot of bottles hidden around to get me through the winter, in the spring I would be able to take my driver training class, I could hardly wait.

Spring came and I finally got to take driver's Ed, I passed it with flying colors, got my permit and shortly after got my licence.I was able to save up enough money from working for farmers, to buy a cheap pickup from one of my neighbors whose father had just passed away and they didn't want the truck around anymore. Now I would be free to come and go where ever I wanted, or at least that is what I thought! My father was getting older he tried very hard to steer me in the right direction. I was becoming out of control with my attitude and my drinking.

I got a work permit and got a part time job at a full service gas station, pumping gas, putting brakes and mufflers on. I started skipping out of school and going up to the gas station, I would just tell my boss I didn't have school that day. My drinking was becoming an everyday thing it was getting out of control, Drinking age was eighteen and nobody carded anyone, if you looked old enough, you could buy it. I always looked older than I was so I never got carded! I started getting in trouble in school being absent so much, the principal called me into his office one day, said I have missed too much school for me to get credit for the school year, and I would have to finish out this year with no credit, go to summer school, and start this grade over next year. Well I sure didn't want no part of that, so I told him there is no way I could do that and got up and walked out.

I had to go back home to pick up some things before I went to work, by the time I got home the principal had already called my dad and told him that I just quit school. Dad was furious, I never seen my father so angry, He told me if I'm not going to go to school, than I can't live under his roof. I was seventeen so I went and told my boss what happened, he was kind of nice to let stay in the back room of the station until I could find a room to rent. My drinking got even worse, I started driving while I was drinking something I never did before. I was bringing girls back to the station to spend the night, something my boss told me not to do. One night while driving I got picked up for driving under the influence (DUI) I spent the night in jail and got a $50 dollar fine they didn't tow my truck because It was parked safely. A few weeks went by and my boss caught me one night with my girlfriend in the back room, after I had closed up the shop. Which he told me when he let me stay there he would not tolerate. He fired me on the spot, that came to me as a shock I thought he would at least give me a second chance, But he didn't. Suddenly it all hit home with me, now I've really done it, I've been kicked out of high school, kicked out of my father's home, lost my job that I dearly loved, got a DUI, lost my girlfriend, and now, I have nowhere to stay. What was I going to to now? What was in store for me next? I started to think that maybe this drinking thing is becoming out of control. Maybe it is time for me to slow way down or even stop drinking for a while. With nowhere else to go I went back to my father, I told him what had happened and that I'm sorry for the things I had done while I was living in his house. I told him I wanted to stop drinking for a while and get a full time job in the day time, and go to adult Ed. At night to get my high school diploma. My Father agreed to those terms and conditions. A Couple weeks went by and I got a full time job in a plastic factory, I was making bathtubs and truck liners. It was very hot! I enrolled in some classes at the adult Ed. four nights a week, so I could graduate in about six months. That kept me very busy so not much time to think about drinking, plus I wanted to prove to myself I could stay off the drinking if I wanted to. Everything went well, no drinking. I was feeling very good about myself. Six months went by fairly fast, then the day came for me to graduate, I walked up on stage and got my diploma, Wow I did it! Now I could just work and maybe go out at night to a movie, or something. I was sure I had the drinking thing under control. That worked for a little while, but then that hideous thought of the first drink came back, one won't hurt, I've been sober for almost eight months now, I will just have one and then stop, that's all nothing more, that should be ok.well that worked for a very short time, with in a couple of months, I was back to drinking every day, but I was only going to drink at home. No more drinking and driving for me, I learned my lesson well. The night in jail was enough for Me. I managed to drink at home for a while, but then I got bored nothing to do no one to talk to, so I started to go out a little how quickly I forget about the horrible night in jail. Then I started to drink at work only during my lunch for a while, then after work on the way home, then before work, It was becoming too much once again. I knew something had to be done about my drinking I'm almost 20 years old and I spend all of my time working and drinking that is all I do, I don't really even have any friends any more.

I started thinking maybe I need to move away from this little home town, go see the world. Become somebody important. I talked it over with my father and mother they thought that it was a very good idea for me to go serve my country, so I decided to join the Navy. That would solve all my problems, as far as drinking was concerned I would be out to sea most of the time, away from alcohol, and I would want to go sightseeing if and when I was in port. So off I went boot camp was three months, I got threw that fairly easy. Then I got orders to go aboard a supply oiler, a ship that goes out to sea for thirty to ninety days at a time and supplies the fleet with goods and cargo, then goes back to nearest port to restock. The first few times in port, it was a whole lot of fun I would go sightseeing and see things I never seen before. I went sightseeing just as I planned.

Then that hideous thought of the first drink came back once again, after that I was drinking very heavy every time the ship went to port, but at least it was only for a week or two at a time. Everything went well for me while I was in the Navy, except for the drinking there was no big trouble. May 1984 I got an honorable discharge from the Navy, I was very proud of myself. I decided to stay on the west coast when I got out of the service, I had a girlfriend at the time there and I loved the weather a whole lot better than that cold Michigan weather. My drinking started up again, but I thought by now I would be able to control it. I would drink for a while then stop, that way I was reassuring myself that I didn't have a drinking problem, I could start and stop any time I wanted to, no problem here. All I really wanted was to be able to drink like other people do. That was my great obsession to be able to drink like other folks. it wasn't too long and my drinking started getting heavy again, so I would cut back on it one more time for a while then stopping for a while. By the mid-eighties I developed a seizure disorder from the large consumption of alcohol, and then suddenly stop. That would put me in the hospital. That really scared me, so each time it would happen I would simply tell myself No more drinking for me that is it, I'm done for good this time! I stayed sober for about one year or so then my girlfriend left me, I couldn't handle it, and I started drinking heavy all over again. The vicious cycle was back on having seizures going to the hospital again. It was a vicious, vicious, cycle. Then 1989 I get picked up for DUI this time it was $ 1000 dollar fine, loss of license for one year and thirty days community service. That vicious cycle continued al threw the nineties, starting and stopping, going to the hospital.1995 I get my third DUI this time it's a lot worse on me, the fine, loss of license, the community service, a year of DUI school, and court ordered into a 12 step program. I sure didn't like that too much, but I went anyway, I had to in order to get my license back, and I had to get a court paper signed for the court.

Most people in 12 step programs introduce themselves as an alcoholic, but one man stood out to me, he introduced himself as someone who has recovered from a hopeless state of mind and body. I liked the sound of that, there was no way I was going to introduce myself as an alcoholic If someone called on me, but I might be able to say I Have recovered. Although I wasn't sure about, from a hopeless state of mind and body. I didn't really even know what that met. I didn't say much, I just got my card signed and left. I was staying sober just fine on my own, Thank You very much! A whole year had passed I was still sober. I could hardly believe it myself. Maybe I have recovered after all.

After I finished My DUI School and got my license back I wanted to have one last hurrah, after I had been sober for a year I'm sure I can control it this time. So I started to drink again, it was only a little for a while, No big deal, right? But then one night I don't know what came over me, all of the sun I was drinking out of control, and I didn't seem to even care, I knew I might have a problem now. But I just couldn't face it right then. A few months went on, this time I really did it, and I was taken to the hospital by ambulance for alcohol overdose. I was on a life support machine for a couple of weeks, when I came to enough to know what was happening, and starting to feel a little better. I was told I had a visitor the nurse ask me if it would be ok if he came in, she said he just wants to talk to you. Not knowing who he was, I said it would be ok but only for a short time. When I looked up to see who it was, I was shocked to see it was the man from the 12 step program I was going to for a while. Remember the man I told you earlier about that I admired. Well He introduced himself as a man who has recovered from a hopeless state of mind and body. OH My God! He told me he works with the hospital on a regular basis, and talks to people who come into the hospital with alcohol and drug problems. Wow! That got my attention! We talked for hours, he shared with me how he was just like me. He also had an alcohol and drug problem and was on a life support machine to. He was just like me at one time. Someone came to his bed side, just like he is doing with me. He said he is only there to help me if I choose to let him. He stayed for a long while talking. Then he gave me his phone number and told me to call him when I get out of the hospital. The next day the Dr released me to go home. But before he did he had this to say to me. The Dr said I am a hopeless chronic alcoholic who will be dead in a few years if I continue. And that I need to get help for my problem now. That hit pretty hard, I went with a large chunk in my throat from what the Dr had said. When I got home, I was all alone and afraid. And not really sure what I should do next, I went to the store and got some more boozes and start drinking again. Then I got really scared my whole life started to pass in front of me.

Knowing only of God, I simply said, God if you are out there please help now, I can't do this alone anymore. I immediately got up and poured the rest of the liquor down the drain. The next day I got out and I went back to that 12 step program, to look for that man I admired so much, and see if he could help me. That was July 10 1998 I haven't had a drink since by the grace of God. I have recovered from a hopeless state of mind and body.

This is how it went.

CHAPTER TWO

Struggling to recover

I met the man I admired and ask him if he could help me recover from a hopeless state of mind and body.

He agreed to help me if he could but I had to be willing to do the work, and it would mean hard honest work.

The first thing I had to do was admit, and acknowledge down deep in my heart that I was an alcoholic. This was not going to be easy for me, I spent years having people tell me that the first step in recovery is to admit it. I might be able to go as far to say I have a serious drinking problem, but that is about as far as I wanted to go. What was I going to do? I had reached the jumping off point. Either I try to block out any conscientious I might have and go to the bitter end, or I start listening to people who have come before me. After struggling with it for a while, and doing some research, I decided once and for all, I am an alcoholic. In fact deep down inside of me, I knew that I was an alcoholic. But I just never could admit it until now. I always thought of an alcoholic, as someone in a long dirty trench coat carrying a brown paper bag. But that is not true, an alcoholic is someone who cannot control their alcohol.so by that definition I am certainly an alcoholic. I tried to prove that I could control my alcohol for years and years.

Suddenly I felt a sense of peace come over me, my friend told me that was the presence of God. I didn't know what it was but it sure felt good. Next I had to admit to myself that I'm powerless over alcohol.

That I did not understand, how am I powerless over it? I'm the one that goes to the store and buys it, I'm the one who twist off the cap, I'm the one who puts it up to my mouth and drinks it, and how am I powerless over it? But then my friend pointed out to me, what happens to me when I do drink it? I can't control how much I drink, or what I do, I have seizures when I drink too much, I end up In the hospital, I lose my license, I have to pay fines, I go to jail, I get a DUI,I have to go to DUI school. Next I had to admit to myself that my life was unmanageable. Again I thought I was doing a pretty good job managing my life. I was able to hold down a job, I was able to go to work every day, how is that unmanageable? Most people don't have the court system tell them where they have to go, and what to do. Most people don't get DUI's and go to the hospital for overdose. Ok so I guess my life is unmanageable. Wow that was a lot to swallow, So Have I recovered from a hopeless state of mind and body now? Well not exactly! There is still a lot of work to do, if I truly want to recover.

Up to this point, I realized I was relying on my own human power, and that wasn't working very well. I knew I had to start focusing on a Spiritual Power much greater than anything I could ever imagine. I had never really been a churchman, but their proposals were not too hard to swallow.

It met I would have to throw several lifelong conceptions out of the window. Lack of power that was my problem.

I had to find a power greater than I had ever known, which I could live with, believe in trust in and learn to love. That was not going to be easy for someone who always believed in self. But I had to go forward and try the best way I could. With help from my friend.

But where and how was I to find this power? I knew that God is everywhere but when you can't see, touch, or hear Him, it makes it a bit difficult. Especially when you have never really tried.

How could a Supreme Being have anything to do with it at all? Then I started thinking, why was I court ordered to a certain place where there was a man I would admire, then why would that same man show up at my bedside, even though we never met before, strange, I don't think so. That was God paving the way for me.Wow! At that moment I got goosebumps.

How could I comprehend a Supreme Being anyhow? Well after that experience how could I not?

As soon as I admitted the possible existence of a Creative Intelligence, a Spirit of the Universe, all powerful of all things, I began to have a new sense of power and direction.

I needed to ask myself but one question.

Do I now believe, or am I even willing to believe, that there is a Spiritual Power greater than myself? Yes! And that spirit is God! In the past I would have been so touchy that even casual reference made me bristle with antagonism.

At this respect alcohol was a great persuader, it finally beat me into a state of reasonableness.

Instead of regarding myself as an intelligent agent, a spearhead of God's advancing Creation.

I chose to believe that my human intelligence was the last word.

Rather vain of me wasn't it?

I would look at the human defects of people, and sometimes use their shortcomings as a basis of wholesale condemnation.

I talked of intolerance, while I was intolerance myself...

I never really gave the spiritual side of life a fair hearing.

I was biased and unreasonable about the realm of the spirit.

When I saw others solve their problems by a simple reliance upon the Spirit of the Universe, I had to stop doubting the power of God.

When I knew in my heart I might be alcoholic, crushed by a self-imposed crisis, I could not postpone or evade.

I had to fearlessly face the proposition that either God is everything, or else He is nothing.

God either is, or He Isn't.

What was my choice to be?

Had I not been brought to where I stood by a certain kind of faith?

Did I not believe in my own reasoning? For years I believed in myself that I could handle anything that came my way. I know now that, that kind of thinking only lead me to drink even more.

Did I not have faith in my ability to think? My thinking was what got me into trouble.

Wasn't that a sort of faith? I only had faith in myself

Had I not variously worshiped people, sentiment, things, money, and myself?

And then with a better motive, had I not worshipfully beheld the sunset, the sea, or a flower?

Who of us had not loved something or somebody?

How much did these feeling, these loves, these worships, have to do with pure reason?

It was impossible to say I had no capacity for faith, or love or worship.

In one form or another I had been living by faith and little else.

Could I really say the whole thing was nothing but a mass of electrons, created out of nothing, meaning nothing whirling on to a destiny of nothingness?

They said God made these things possible, and I only smiled.

I had seen spiritual release, but told myself it wasn't true.

I am fooling myself, for deep down in every man woman, and child, there is the fundamental idea of God. I finally saw that faith in some kind of God was a part of my make-up after all, just as much as the feeling I have for a friend.

"Who am I to say there is no God?"

I humbly offered myself to God as I knew him.

God had restored me to sanity.

He has come to all who have honestly sought Him.

CHAPTER THREE
Surrendering

The first requirement is that I had to be convinced that any life run on self-will can hardly be a success.

Admitting I may be at fault, but I was sure that other people were more to blame.

I became angry, indignant, self-pitying.

What was my basic trouble? Self-centered, Selfishness

Am I just really a self-seeker, even trying to be kind? Even though I was kind most of the time, true story is I was only seeking your kindness back so I could get something to benefit me.

Am I just a victim of the delusion, that I could just have satisfaction, and happiness out of this would, if I only manage better? I became a manipulator, without even realizing it.

Is not evident to all the rest of the world that these are the things I want? Trying to be the director, I just wanted everyone to follow my cue.

But my actions only make them wish to retaliate? When things would not go my way, I would get angry, causing you to retaliate. Even in my best moments.

Am I just a producer of confusion rather than harmony? A perfect example of self will run riot.

Are not most of us concerned with ourselves, our resentments, or self-pity? Because I was caught up in self, I wanted to believe everybody thought the same way I did It didn't allow me to think of anyone else the way God would prefer me to.

Selfishness-self-centeredness! That I think is the root of all of my troubles.

Driven by hundreds of forms of fear, self-delusion, self-seeking,

And self-pity I would step on the toes of my fellows.

So my troubles are basically of my own making.

Above everything, I must be rid of this selfishness or it will kill me!

He is my Father and I am his child.

God I offer myself to Thee-to build with me and to do with me as Thou wilt. Relieve me of bondage of self, that I may better do Thy will. Take away my difficulties, that victory over them may bear witness to those I would help of Thy Power, Thy love, and Thy way of life. May I always do Thy will, your will be done not mine Amen.

I had to make sure I was ready, before I could at last abandon myself to God.

I had to make sure I was expressing the idea, voicing it without reservation.

It could have little permanent effort to face, and be rid of, the things in myself which had been block

CHAPTER FOUR
Taking a Hard Look

A business which takes no regular inventory usually goes broke.

Inventory is a fact-finding fact-facing process.

It is an effort to discover the truth.

One object is to disclose damaged goods, to get rid of them promptly and without regret.

The business owner cannot fool himself about values.

I had to do exactly the same things with my live, I took stock of myself honestly.

First I searched out the flaws in my make-up which caused my failure?

Being convinced that self, manifested in various ways what had defeated me? Pride, Selfishness, Self-Centered, Anger, Fear, Envy, Greed, Gluttony, Sloth and Lust I considered its common manifestations.

Resentment is the "number one" offender it destroys more alcoholics than anything else.

From it, stem all forms of spiritual disease.

I have been not only mentally and physically ill, I have been spiritually sick.

In dealing with my resentments, I set them on paper.

I listed the people, institutions, or principles with whom I was angry,

I ask myself why I was angry.

In most cases it was found that my self-esteem, my pocketbooks, my ambitions, my personal relationships were hurt or threatened.

I went back through my live, nothing counted but thoroughness and honesty, when I was finished, and I considered it carefully. The first thing parent was that this world and its people were often quite wrong.

To conclude that others were wrong was as far as I had got.

The usual outcome was that people continued to wrong me and I stayed sore.

Sometimes it was remorse and then I was sore at myself.

The more I fought and tried to have my own way the worse matters got.

It is plain that a life which includes deep resentment leads only to futility and unhappiness.

When harboring such feeling I shut myself out from the sunlight of the Spirit.

The insanity of alcohol returns again.

I turned back to my list, for it held the key to the future.

I began to see that the world and its people really dominated me.

How could I escape? At this point! I had to write out what disturbed me about each person on my list.

I saw that these resentments must be mastered At once, I had to talk to someone about all of this I wrote down. Referring back to my list again.

Putting out of my mind the wrongs others had done, I resolutely looked for my own mistakes.

Where had I been selfish, dishonest, self-seeking and frightened?

Where was I to blame?

The word fear somehow touches about every aspect of my live.

It sets in motion trains of circumstances which brought me misfortune I felt I didn't deserve.

But did not I, myself, set the ball rolling?

I ask myself why I had them.

Was it because self-reliance had failed me?

At one time I had great self-confidence, but it didn't fully solve the fear problem.

When it made me cocky it was worse.

Perhaps there is a better way.

For now I am on a different basis; the basis of trusting and relying upon God.

I trust infinite God rather than myself.

I am in the world to play the role He assigns.

I ask Him to remove my fear and direct my attention to what He would have me be.

I looked over my own conduct over the years.

Where had I been selfish, dishonest, or inconsiderate?

Whom had I hurt, did I unjustifiably arouse jealousy, suspicion or bitterness?

Where was I at fault, what should I have done instead?

I got this all down on paper and looked at it.

In this way I tried to shape a sane and sound idea for my future. I ask God to mold my ideals and help me to live up to them.

Whatever my ideal turns out to be, I must be willing to grow toward it.

I must be willing to make amends where I had done harm, provided that I do not bring about more harm in so doing,

In meditation, I ask God what I should do about each specific matter. The right answer will come, if I truly want it.

God alone can judge my situation.

Counsel with another person is often desirable, but I let God be the final judge.

If I have already made a decision, and an inventory of my grosser handicaps, than I have made a good beginning.

That being so I have swallowed and digested some big chunks of truth about myself.

I have been trying to get a new attitude, a new relationship with my Creator, and to discover the obstacles in my path. I have admitted certain defects; I have ascertained in a rough way what the trouble is; I have put my finger on the weak items in my personal inventory.

CHAPTER FIVE
Admitting To God

If I skip out on admitting to God.to myself, and to another person the nature of my wrongs, than I may not recover.

I cannot allow myself to turn to easier methods, I take inventory all right but hang on to some of the worst items in stock, and I knew I had to be Honest, Fearless, and Thorough.

Sometimes I feel like I lead a double life, I am much like an actor.to the outer world I present my stage character.

This is the one I like my fellows to see.

I want to enjoy a certain reputation, but I know in my heart I don't deserve it.

I push these memories inside myself, in hopes they never see the light of day. I am under constant fear and tension.

I must be entirely honest with somebody if I expect to live long or happily in this world.

Rightly and naturally, I had to think well before I choose the person or persons with whom to take this intimate and confidential step. I cannot disclose anything to someone which will hurt them.

I had to pocket my pride and go right to it, illuminating every twist of character, every dark cranny of the past. Once I have done that, withholding nothing, I am delighted I can look the world in the eye!

I can be alone at perfect peace and ease.

My fears fall from me, I began to feel the nearness of my Creator. Now I begin to have a spiritual experience that feeling that the drink problem has disappeared.

I feel I am on the Broad Highway, walking hand and hand with the Spirit of the Universe.

CHAPTER SIX
One with God

Returning home I find a place where I can be quiet for an hour, carefully reviewing what I have done.

I thank my God from the bottom of my heart that I know Him better.is my work solid so far? Are the stones properly in place? Have I skimped on the cement put into the foundation? Have I tried to make mortar without sand?

Am I now ready to let God remove from me all the things which I have admitted are objectionable?

Can he now take them all-every one?

I humbly ask Him to remove my shortcomings.

My Creator, I am now willing that you should have all of me good and bad I pray that you now remove from me every single defect of character which stands in the way of my usefulness to you and my fellows. Lord grant me strength, as I go out from here, to do your bidding.

Amen

Suddenly I feel a sense of peace come over me, like a cool mountain breeze of fresh air. But I know there is more work that needs to be done, without it I find that "Faith without works is dead"

I still have my list of all people I had harmed and to whom I am willing to make amends to, the one I made when I took inventory.

I subjected myself to a drastic self-appraisal.

Now I must go out to the people I have done harm to and repair the damage, I did in the past.

I attempt to sweep away all the bad, which has accumulated out of my effort to live on self-will and run the show myself. But if I don't have the will at any given time, I spend time with my Creator and ask for it to come. There are some misgivings, as I look back over the list of business acquaintances and friends I have hurt, I feel diffident about going to some of them on a spiritual basis. To some people I need not and probably should not, I might prejudice them.

My real purpose is to fit myself to be of maximum service to God and people about us.

It is seldom wise to approach an individual, who still smarts from my injustice.

Why lay myself open to being branded fanatics or religious bores?

They may be more interested in a demonstration of good will, than in my talk of spiritual discoveries.

The question of how to approach the man, I felt hate to will arise. It may be he has done me more harm than I have done him, and though I may have acquired a better attitude toward him, I am still not too great about admitting my faults. It is harder to go to an enemy than to a friend, but I find if much more beneficial to me.

Nevertheless, I always try to go to him in a helpful and forgiving spirit.

Under no condition do I ever criticize such a person.

Simply I tell him that I will never get over drinking until I have done my utmost best to straighten out the past.

I am there to sweep off my side of the street.

I must go to any lengths to find a spiritual experience.

The alcoholic is like a tornado, roaring his way through the lives of others. Hearts are broken, sweet relationships are dead. Affections have been uprooted.

Selfish and inconsiderate habits have kept the home in turmoil.

A remorseful mumbling that I am sorry won't fill the bill at all. In my meditation I ask my Creator to show me the way of patience, tolerance, kindness and love to all.

The spiritual life is not a theory, I have to live it.

Some people that cannot be seen, I send them an honest letter. I must always be sensible, tactful, and considerate and humble.

As God's people I stand on my feet; I don't crawl before anyone. I found that I was amazed before I was halfway through. I felt as if I was going to know a new freedom and a new happiness. And I began to know peace. I started to lose interest in selfish things and gain interest in other people.my whole attitude and outlook upon life has changed. I suddenly realized that God is doing for me what I could not do for myself.

CHAPTER SEVEN
Continue to look at myself

I continue to set right any mistakes as I go along. I must began to live this way of life, if I don't I could drift back into my old way of life.

I have entered into the world of the Spirit.

My next function is to grow in understanding. And effectiveness, and it should continue for the rest of my life time.

I need to always watch for selfishness, dishonesty, and fear. When these crop up, I ask God immediately and make amends quickly. Then I turn my thoughts to someone I can help. I have ceased fighting anything or anyone even alcohol. By this time sanity has returned, I am seldom

Interested in alcohol, if I am tempted, I ask God at once to take the temptation away.

I have seen that my new attitude toward alcohol has been given to me without any thought or effort on our part.

I am not fighting it, neither am I avoiding temptation.

I feel as if I have been put in a position of neutrality-safe and protected. The problem has been removed, it does not exist for me I am not afraid.

That is how I react so long as I keep in fit spiritual condition.it Is easy to let up on the spiritual program of action and rest on our laurels, I am headed for trouble if I do. I am not cured of alcoholism. What I have is a daily reprieve, contingent on the maintenance of my spiritual condition. Every day is a day when I must carry the vision of God's will into all my activities.

CHAPTER EIGHT
Prayer and Meditation

I shouldn't be shy on this matter of payer, I try to spend twenty minutes in the morning and twenty minutes at night and I give thanks to my Lord all through the day.

It works if I have the proper attitude and work it.

When I retire at night, I constructively review my day.

Was I resentful, selfish, dishonest, or afraid? Do I owe an apology? Have I kept something to myself which should be?

Discussed with another person at once? Was I kind and loving toward all?

What could I have done better? Was I thinking of myself most of the time? Or was I thinking of what I could do for others, of what could I pack into the stream of life? But I must be careful not to drift into worry, or remorse. That would diminish my usefulness to others. After making my review I ask God to forgive me, and inquire what corrective measures should be taken?

On awakening I think about the twenty four hours ahead. I consider my plans for the day, before I begin I ask God to direct my thinking especially asking that it be divorced from self-pity, dishonest or self-seeking motives. I ask God for inspiration, an intuitive thought or decision.

Being still inexperienced and having just made conscious contact with God, it is not probable that I am going to be inspired at all times. I find that my thinking will, as time passes, be more and more on the plane of inspiration. I pray to be shown what my next step is to be. That I be given whatever I need to take care of such problems, I ask for freedom from self-will.

It helps to select and memorize a few set of prayers which emphasize the principles.

One Prayer that is very easy to memorize and is used by a lot of people is

> God grant me the Serenity to accept
> The things I cannot change....
> Courage to change the things
> I can...and the Wisdom to know

The Difference.

I say this prayer throughout the day every day. Another very good Prayer to say and absorb whenever I'm feeling down is the Peace Prayer

> Peace Prayer of Saint Francis
>
> Lord make me an instrument of your peace;
> Where there is hatred, let me sow love;
> Where there is injury, pardon;
> Where there is doubt, faith;

Where there is despair, hope;
Where is darkness light?
Where there is sadness, joy;
O divine Master, grant that
I may not so much seek to
Be consoled to console,
To be understood as to understand,
To be loved as to love
For it is in giving that
We receive, it is in pardoning
That we are pardoned,
And it is in dying that we are
Born to eternal life.
Amen

As I go through the day I pause, when agitated or doubtful, and ask for the right thought or action. I constantly remind myself I am no longer running the show, humbly saying to myself.

"Thy will be done" not mine

We alcoholics are undisciplined people, so we let God discipline us.

CHAPTER NINE
Helping Others

My Experience shows that nothing will so much insure immunity from drinking as intensive work with another alcoholic, or someone who feels blocked from the Holy Spirit. It works when other activities fail.

I can help when no one else can, can secure their confidence when others fail. Life will take on new meaning, to watch people recover, to watch loneliness vanish. Frequent contact with others is the bright spot of my live. Because of my own drinking experience I can be uniquely useful to other alcoholics. To be helpful is my only aim.

If a person does not want to stop drinking I don't waste my time trying to persuade him. I can get an idea of his behavior, his problems, his background, the seriousness of his condition, and his religions learning. I don't deal with him when he is very drunk, unless he is ugly and the family needs my help.

I tell him enough about my drinking habits, symptoms, and experiences to encourage him to speak of himself.

I Tell him how baffled I was, how I finally learned I was sick. I try to tell him of the struggles I had to stop, I try to explain to him the mental twist which leads to the first drink. If he is an alcoholic,

31

he will understand me at once. Then I Begin to tell him of the hopelessness of alcohol.

I am always careful not to label him as an alcoholic, I let him draw his own conclusion. If he still thinks he can control his drinking, I let him know perhaps he can if he is not to alcoholic. But I let him know if he is too affected by alcohol, there may be little to no chance he can recover by himself.

I talk to him about alcoholism how it is a fatal disease. I let him know about the conditions of mind which accompany it. I Explain that many are doomed who never realize it.

I talk to him about the hopelessness of alcoholism as long as I offer a solution. I let him know exactly what happened to me, I always Stress the spiritual feature.

If the man be agnostic or atheist, I make it clear he does not have to agree with my conception of God.as long as he is willing to believe in a Power greater than himself, and that he live by spiritual principles. There is no use arousing any prejudice he may have against certain theological terms about which he may already be confused.

His religious education and training may be far superior to mine.

Faith must be accompanied by self-sacrifice and unselfish, constructive, maybe I have disturbed him about the question of alcoholism, this is all for the good. The more hopeless he feels, the better, he will be more likely to follow my suggestions. He may rebel at the thought of housecleaning, which requires discussion with another person. I tell him I once felt as he does, but I doubt I would have made much progress had I not taken action.

I never talk down to an alcoholic or anyone from a moral or spiritual hilltop, I simply lay out the kit of spiritual tools for his inspection. I tell him if he wants to get well I will do anything to help. If he expects me to act only as a banker for his financial difficulties or a nurse for his sprees, I may have to drop him. He must decide for himself whether he wants to go on. He should not be pushed or probed by me, his wife, or his friends, if he is going to find God, the desire must come from within.

I find it a waste of time to keep chasing a man who cannot or will not work with me.If I leave him alone, he may soon become convinced that he cannot recover by himself I depart as friends.

To spend too much time on any one situation is to deny some other alcoholic or other person an opportunity to live and be happy.

I let him know I am available if he wishes to make a decision and tell his story, but I do not insist upon it if he prefers to consult someone else. He may be broke and homeless, if he is, I might try to help him about getting a job, or give him a little financial assistance. But I do not deprive my family or creditors of money they should have. Perhaps I will want to take the man into my home for a few days, But I have to be sure I use discretion, I always have to be certain he will be welcomed by my family, and that he is not trying to impose upon me for money, connections or shelter.

I never avoid these responsibilities, but I have to be sure I am doing the right thing if I assume them.

Helping others is the foundation stone of my recovery.

A kind act once in a while isn't enough. It may mean the loss of many nights sleep, interference with my pleasures, interruptions to my business.it may mean sharing my home and my money.

Counseling frantic wife's and relatives, trips to the police station,courts,sanitariums,hospitals,jails and asylums.my telephone may ring at any time of the day or night.

A drunk may smash some furniture in my home, or burn a hole in a mattress, I may have to fight with him if he becomes violent. Sometimes I may have to call the police or an ambulance. Sometimes these things may happen.

I usually don't allow an alcoholic to live in my home for a long time, it is not good for him, and it can create complication in the family.

The alcoholic who is able and willing to get well, little charity, in the sense of the word, is needed or wanted.

The men who cry for money and shelter before conquering alcohol, are on the wrong path.

It is not the matter of giving that is the question, but when and how much to give. I have to be sure he is relying on God and not on me. He may be divorced, or separated, I will try to help him. Explain his new principles by which he is living to his family. He should concentrate on his own spiritual demonstration, and never argue or try to find fault with them.

This may be a difficult thing to do, but it must be done if he expects any results. After a time the family will see how well it is working for him and perhaps want to go along. However sometimes it is to the best interests of all concerned that the couple remain apart.

Sometimes I have to Remind him his recovery is not dependent on other people, it is dependent on his relationship with God.

When I look back, I realize that the things which came to me when I put myself in God's hands were far better than anything I could have imagined. Follow the way of the Lord and you will live in a new and wonderful world, no matter what the circumstances!

When I'm working with a man and his family I do not participate in there quarrels, I may spoil my chance of being helpful. I try to explain to them that his defects of character are not going away overnight. I try to show them he has entered into a period of growth, and I encourage them to try to grow with him.

As long as I'm spiritual fit I can do all sorts of things.

I don't avoid a place where there is drinking, if I have good reason for being there. I just ask myself on each occasion, have I good social, business, or personal reason for going to that place? Or am I expecting to steal a little pleasure from the atmosphere of that place? I have to be honest with myself

I do not think of what I can get out of the place.

I Think about what I can bring to it.Why sit with a long face in places where alcohol is being serviced, sighing about the good old days.

My friends or business acquaintances, should not have to change their habits on my account. At a proper time I can explain to them why I don't drink. While I was drinking I was withdrawing from life little by little.

Now I am getting back into the social life again. I don't want to start to withdraw again just because my friends drink alcohol.my job now is to be at the place where I can be of maximum helpfulness to others, so I never hesitate to go anywhere if I can be helpful. If

I keep on this track of life with these motives and God will keep me safe.

I am careful never to show intolerance or hatred of drinking, such an attitude is not helpful to anyone.

CHAPTER TEN
Working with the Wifes

For every man who drinks others are involved the wife who trembles in fear of their husband, the mother or father who see their child wasting their lives away.

As wives of the alcoholic I want you to feel that I understand as perhaps no others can I want to leave You with the feeling that no situation is too difficult and no unhappiness too great to overcome. I understand you have traveled a rocky road, with hurt pride, frustration, self-pity, misunderstanding and fear.

You have been driven to sympathy, bitter resentment and from one extreme to another extreme. Always hoping your husband would be himself once more. I know you have been unselfish and self-sacrificing, telling numerous lies to protect your pride and your husband's reputations. You have prayed, begged, been patient, and have even ran away.

Your homes were battlegrounds many days and nights,

Always hoping. You seldom had friends over to your house, in fear of how your husband would react. You would make few social engagements, you came to live almost alone. When you would go out your husband would sneak so many drinks it would spoil the party.

There was never any financial security, the checking account melted like snow. The bill collectors, the police, the angry cab drivers, the bums, the pals, and even other women he brought home.

The next day you would forgive and try to forget. Than to enter the final stage which met hospitals, heath farms, or jail, you knew death was near. You would ask yourselves how someone who loves his wife could and children be so unthinking, so callous, and so cruel? And just when you were convinced of their heartlessness, they would surprise you and be their self again, only to tear it all down again.

Then you would wonder if they did not love their family, how could they be so blind about themselves? What had become of their judgment, their common sense, and their will power? How could they not see that drink was to mean ruin to them? Why was it, when these dangers were pointed out to them and they agreed, then they got drunk all over again?

You can see that when he is not drinking, he loves you dearly, but when he drinks he is unloving and inconsiderate.

Is it right to let him ruin your life and your children's life?

Or maybe your husband is only a heavy drinker,

His drinking may be all the time or only on certain occasions, he spends a lot of money on liquor, slowing him down mentally and physically. Sometimes he is an embarrassment to you and his friends. But he is sure he can handle his liquor, that it doesn't hurt him. Or maybe drinking is necessary in his line of work, He would get insulted if someone called him an alcoholic. Or maybe your husband is showing lack of control, he is unable to stop even if he wants to. He gets out of hand when drinking, he admits this is true, but insist he will do better next time. He tries different ways to moderate or stay dry, maybe he is starting to lose his friends, or perhaps his business is hurting, he begins to worry that maybe he just can't drink like other people. Maybe he drinks in the morning to calm his nerves, and all through the day.

Maybe he gets worse, his friends have all slipped away, the home is near-wreck and he cannot hold a job.

He starts to admit he can't control his liquor, but does not understand. Your husband may be too far gone, he has been in one institution after another. He is violent when drinking, often times he drinks on the way home from the hospital, or jail. Many alcoholics have been much worse than this, but with the proper help from a trusted friend, and the grace of God they got better.

First thing is try not to get angry, even if he is unbearable and you have to leave him?

Patience and kindness are what matters most, never tell him what he must do about his drinking, he needs to realize that on his own. Your husband's drinking should not ruin your relationship with your children or your friends.

They need your companionship as much as you need theirs, you can still have a useful and happy life even though your husband is still drinking. Pray for him that he will see how his drinking has destroyed him, the power of God goes deep! He may soon come around and seek help, but keep in mind some men never do recover.

As your husband begins recovery on a spiritual principle, you may find it promising to build your character along with him, also on a spiritual principle.

All problems will not be solved at once, In spite of your new found happiness. There will still be ups and downs.

Some of the old problems and attitudes will still be with you. Faith of both you and your husband will be tested, as you grow and learn to live a new way of life.

You may make many mistakes, but if you are Faithful, they will not bring you down, and a better way of life will emerge.

You may experience some irritation, hurt feeling, resentment, your husband may be unreasonable, and you will want to criticize him.

This is very dangerous especially to your husband, often times you may have to carry the burdens, or avoiding them, or at least keeping them under control.(remember God's will not mine) this does not mean you have to agree when there is an honest difference of opinion, just be careful not to disagree in a resentful or critical spirit.

Next time there is a heated discussion, you or your husband should take the privilege, to smile and say, this is getting serious. I'm sorry I got disturbed, let's talk about this later. If you and your husband are trying to live on a spiritual basis, this will avoid disagreement. Your husband knows he owes you more than just sobriety, but try not to expect too much. Patience, tolerance, understanding and love are extremely essential. Show him these things in yourself and they will reflect back to you. If you both show a willingness to remedy your own defects, there will be hardly nothing to criticize about. You may become jealous of the attention he gets from working with other alcoholics, you have been starving for his companionship, yet he spends most of his time helping others. You may feel as if he should now be yours, Fact is he has to work with others to maintain his own sobriety. Sometimes he may even become neglectful.

Your house may be filled with people you don't know, and some of which you may not like. He seems to be more concerned about their troubles, and not concerned about yours. But it will do him or you no good if you point it out to him and demand more attention for yourself. Instead you should try to join in his efforts as much as you can, maybe get involved with the wives of his new found friends. After all you both have a lot in common.

Both you and your husband should be thinking about what you can put into life, instead of how much you can take out. By doing so you will find you and he have a much fuller, better and happier life.

I understand, I have spoken a lot about the wife, and may seem that I have lectured. If that is so I'm sorry, I don't like it when someone tries to lecture me only speak of my own experience, some of which may be painful, I am anxious to help you understand, so you can avoid these unnecessary difficulties. My only goal is to be of Maximum service to my Creator. My only aim is to be helpful.

CHAPTER ELEVEN
Comforting the Children

The children may have the impression that Dad may be wrapped in white cotton, and be placed on a pedestal. If Dad is going to be successful than that is not true. All family members should be on common ground, of tolerance, understanding, and love. The family may have their own fixed ideas of Dads attitude. Each one of them might expect to have their own wishes met. This will mean for dysfunction and unhappiness. Somehow they long for the good old days, and security of their father, when he was so kind, loving, thoughtful and successful, But when he falls short, than the family becomes unhappy. Father knows he is to blame; it may take many years to restore what he has damaged over the years. But the family should admire him for what he is trying to become, rather than what is not.

We grow by our willingness to face our past, our mistakes, and turn them into assets.

Father may plunge into a frantic attempt to make up for lost time, in business, to solve his money problems. The family may feel pleasant about this at first, then they find themselves neglected, Dad may be too tired after a long day, and too busy during the day. He may take little interest in the children, and show irritation at their approach for him to spend more time with them. Or he may seem dull, and boring, not a whole lot of fun to be around. Mother may complain of the lack of attention, he has been giving, they may all be disappointed and often let him know about it, this can bring up barriers.

He is striving to recover and make up for lost time, he feels as though he is doing very well, although mother and children don't think so. Having been neglected in the past because of his drinking, they think father owes them more than they are getting. They want him to show more interest in them, they expect him to give them the good times they used to have before he started drinking too much. But Dad doesn't give so freely of himself, resentments start to happen, he becomes even less communicative. The family is mystified, they began to criticize him pointing out how he is falling down on his spiritual ways. This kind of thing can be avoided, both father and the family are mistaken.

The family must realize that Dad. Has improved a great deal, but is still learning a great amount. They should try to be grateful that he is finally sober at last. Let them remember that his drinking has done a lot of damage over the years, and may take a long time to repair. If they sense these things then they can try to be more patience when dad is cranky, or depressed, which will go away in time. Love tolerance, and spiritual understanding. Dad must see the danger of over trying on his success. He is not likely to get too far in any direction, if he fails to show unselfishness, love, tolerance, and spiritual understanding to his family.

Giving rather than getting will become the guiding principle. On the other hand Dad may become a religious enthusiast, he is unable to focus on anything else. This may cause the family to look at their dad as a stranger, which cause irritation. He talks of spiritual things all through the day and into the night. He may be a little pushy, and demanding that the family find God and in a hurry. Perhaps the family has been religious their whole life, He may tell them they don't know what it's all about, and they better get his brand of spirituality before it is too late. This can cause the family to be jealous of a God who has stolen their Dad's affection. They are grateful he don't drink any more, but don't like the idea that God has done this miracle where they had failed. They often forget dad was beyond human aid. They may not be able to see why their love didn't straighten him out. They may wonder if Dad is so spiritual, and wants to make right his wrongs, why he seems to care for everybody else in the world but not his own family.

What about his talk that God will provide for them? They start to think Dad is a little off balance. Father feels as if he has struck Gold, he wants to keep it all to himself for a time. If the family cooperates, Dad will soon see he is suffering from a distortion of valves. He will soon see his spiritual growth is a bit lopsided. If the family can realize dad's behavior is just a phase of his development, all will be well. The father, mother, and family should absolutely insist on having fun, God didn't make us to be unhappy people!

MY MESSAGE

I speak of alcohol a lot in this book, because it was alcohol that blocked me from knowing and serving God, the Lord Jesus Christ. But many things can block us humans from the sun light of the Spirit. If you or someone you know is struggling, and feel blocked from the Spirit. Just substitute what that is with the alcohol and it will work the same way. I tried to lay out a plan how to take a look at yourself and work through it. I hope this book has been helpful. Maybe we will meet up on the Broad Highway as we walk hand and hand with our God. May God Bless You And Keep You.

Until Then,
Donald Milbocker

Printed in the United States
By Bookmasters